The
Christian Father

by
Keith Chappell

*All booklets are published thanks to the
generous support of the members of the
Catholic Truth Society*

CATHOLIC TRUTH SOCIETY
PUBLISHERS TO THE HOLY SEE

Contents

All rights reserved. First published 2008 by The Incorporated Catholic Truth Society 40-46 Harleyford Road, London SE11 5AY Tel: 020 7640 0042 Fax: 020 7640 0046. Copyright © 2008 The Incorporated Catholic Truth Society.

ISBN 978 1 86082 514 9

Introduction

"The thing is", Sylvia said as she tried to blink back her tears, "you can have several dads during your life but you only have one mother". Sylvia was discussing her faith, particularly her anger with God, in light of the recent death of her mother. Through this one simple phrase I became instantly distracted from our task of exploring the Sacrament of Confirmation, which Sylvia was preparing for as one of the many adults who miss this great sacrament as a young person. My own role as a husband and father had defined the previous twelve years of my life. Could I be so dispensable in the lives of my children? Is being a father simply a matter of being the partner of a child's mother? True, Sylvia was simply trying to emphasize the unique role of a mother in our lives and was, perhaps, reflecting upon her lack of a close relationship with her own father following her mother's remarriage. However, the fact that she felt it was acceptable to say this and that nothing in her wider experience had suggested that there might be a special, even unique, position for fathers touches upon a deeper problem in our society. What does it mean to be a father in the twenty-first century? More importantly, for our purposes here, what does it mean to be the father of a Catholic family in a society that throws so many new challenges at us and our children?

What it means to be a father is something that has exercised the minds of many great thinkers from before the ancient Greeks right up to the present day. It is a question that has led to many books and spawned a number of organisations, particularly over the last few decades. We too in our turn take a look at what a father is, and has been through history, before going on to look at what the Church says about fatherhood and how a Christian father can live his mission.

It is not the purpose of this booklet to tell the reader how to be a father; it is hard to think of anything more alienating than someone telling you how to live your most intimate relationships. When your first child is on its way it is astounding how many people say something along the lines of "They don't come with an instruction manual". I did notice that nobody seemed to say this to my wife, perhaps the assumption is that the "manual" is built in for mothers. This booklet cannot be, and would never seek to be, the "manual" for fathers, but perhaps it will lead you to reflect on your role as a father and to become aware of the huge internal resources each father has which are given by the grace of the one Father we all look to.

As in Sylvia's case, it is often only in times of loss that we truly examine what something is and what its true value is. In many ways the whole process of mourning is shaped by coming to terms with the lost opportunities, past or future, that come about when a loved one dies. Sadly, relationships often come to an end, and divorce is a reality in the lives of many people today. Couples are becoming increasingly aware of the implications of separation for their children and many are using mediation, rather than the courts, to work out the best arrangements for their children and finances.

The process is emotionally fraught and many, if not most, couples will shed tears at some point in the process. In my experience men are as likely to cry as women but whilst women will cry over a range of issues, including matters of finance and property, men tend to cry over discussions around the children. Why is this? It is likely that people cry in these situations when they feel powerless or vulnerable. Women are often disadvantaged financially through divorce, but men often feel that their role as father is undervalued and that they will lose their relationship with their children. Often men who have not been very "hands-on" fathers during the marriage suddenly, and genuinely, realise the gift that has been given to them through fatherhood. There is, however, an important question raised by this insecurity of fathers: why has fatherhood become so devalued in society when historically it is portrayed as a central, if not the central, relationship in each person's life?

The Loving Father and the Prodigal Son

Running out to greet the son

Many ancient texts, not least the Bible, are full of stories about fatherhood. Indeed, the whole of Scripture is one story of a loving and forgiving Father who constantly strives to bring home His wayward children. He does this by coming to them in many ways: through the Law of Moses; through the prophets; through the wise teachings of the sages; finally, he sends His Son. Fatherhood, as seen in our Father in heaven, is not something that is distant but is loving and nurturing in a way that we often associate only with motherhood in our modern society. To lose sight of this is a tragedy which has implications for parents and their children in today's increasingly fractured society and also for our understanding of God and His calling for us all.

In the Gospel, one of Christ's greatest examinations of the meaning of fatherhood is found in the parable of the prodigal son (*Lk* 15:11-32). This parable is less about the wayward son who wanders off to live a life of debauchery than it is about the father who gives to him freely and welcomes him back unconditionally. The parable is often more rightly called the story of the loving father, and when this is done we can see that it is a summary of the whole of Scripture and of God's love for all of His children. True, this is a story that is simplified in many ways when we consider the complexities of relationships between father and children. In this parable the father is without fault, something no human father should ever delude himself that he can say! Nonetheless it is a parable that calls us to follow the example given and to run out to greet our child with open arms and kisses just as the father in the story runs to his returning son. Fatherhood is not something that just is, nor is it something our children give us; it is something that fathers do and live and, ultimately, give to their children without any expectation of reward. We will return to this parable later.

A changing role, or one that endures?

Fatherhood comes in many forms, and always has. Throughout history children have been separated from one or both parents through death, poverty or marriage breakdown. The result has been that fathers and mothers were often adoptive. Until relatively recently the adult in a single parent family was more likely to be the father than the mother due to high mortality rates during childbirth and divorce laws which assumed the father to be the best custodian of children on financial grounds. There is significant evidence than many of these men did not rely on female relatives or servants for childcare but provided a nurturing environment on their own. In her book *Fatherhood Reclaimed* Adrienne Burgess provides a very good potted survey of fatherhood through history and in different societies. She concludes that fatherhood is not defined by some form of biological pre-programming but is expressed in many different forms depending upon the society and the needs of the individual family involved.

Work-life balance

In the context of western societies, the experience of fatherhood in small agricultural communities where mothers and fathers lived and worked in the same place alongside their children, and cared for them together, was radically overturned by the industrial revolution. The need to work away from home separated both parents, but especially fathers, from their children and disrupted family life. It was partly this disruption of family life that led Leo XIII to publish his encyclical *Rerum novarum* (The Condition of Labour) in 1891. In this encyclical Leo XIII argued for a living wage for workers in what was perhaps one of the first attempts to address the issue of 'work/life balance'. Unfortunately this call was not heeded by wider society and men became increasingly seen as fulfilling their role as fathers through earning money. The role of being with children and caring for them became increasingly identified with mothers, and women generally. This became reinforced over the decades until by the middle of the twentieth century motherhood and the workplace were seen as mutually exclusive with many employers requiring women to leave work on getting married or becoming pregnant. 'Bringing home the bacon' was the task of men and fatherhood had effectively been reduced to providing a roof over the family's heads and putting food on the table.

The issue of work/life balance is more pressing today than ever and Leo XIII would perhaps be more shocked now than he was in 1891. There have been many social and legal developments in recent years to help make it easier for parents, and others such as those caring for elderly or disabled relatives, to balance the demands of work with those of looking after others. It is now a legal right to ask for, but not necessarily to get, flexible working patterns if you have young children under six years old. Fathers now have a right to ask for paternity leave on the birth of a child, but again there are significant restrictions on this. There can be no doubt that it is legally and socially more difficult for fathers to address the balance of work and life; paternity leave tends to be about two weeks whilst maternity leave is generally six months or more. Society accepts that young children need their mothers but is less realistic about the importance of fathers. On one level the concept of work/life balance is a very positive thing; not least because the very name implies that work is not life, it is not what we are made for. There is a risk, however, that we will expect the balancing to come from outside ourselves and outside our family. Waiting for society to change to allow us to spend more time with our children is not only likely to take a long time but it misses the point and means we fail to take on our personal responsibility as parents. It is by spending more time with our children, which may mean making financial or career sacrifices, that we will help to change society. Not least amongst the changes will be its image of fatherhood, and perhaps with that its image of God.

Fatherhood and the Church

Is it as simple as that? Are modern fathers often distant from their children simply because of the pattern of work in modern society? Of course not. Throughout history, and from culture to culture, the role of fathers has shown immense diversity. This is the point made by the impact of the industrial revolution, fatherhood has never been a static thing in the way it is lived even if its essence is rooted in the one fatherhood of God. We can see this shift and development even within the imagery used by the Church to portray fatherhood.

One of the great joys of life in the Catholic Church today is the growth in the reception of adults into communion with the Church through the Rite of Christian Initiation of Adults. Grown men and women come to faith in Christ in maturity and often provide wonderful challenges and questions which force existing Catholics to reflect on their faith in more depth. One area of confusion or misunderstanding for many enquirers is the role of the Blessed Virgin in the life of the Church. Discussing doctrines and dogma can sometimes deepen this confusion but I often find that dwelling on Marian devotion helps to reveal the mysteries held within. For example, in praying the Rosary we soon find that the focus is not Mary but Christ and His life, death and resurrection. Another useful thing to do is to use the many visual aids provided in the Church such as icons and statues.

One evening I was looking at images and statues of Mary in our parish church with Steve, an enquirer in his thirties with two children. He had been very interested in various pictures and icons such as that of Our Lady of Perpetual Succour and a small statue of Mary Mother of God and seemed quite happy with it all. He was, however, troubled by a larger statue of the Immaculate Conception in the Lady Chapel, and stood looking at it for a while. "It doesn't make sense without the baby" he eventually said. Somewhat taken aback by this insight all I could say was "No, none of this makes any sense without the baby". Our whole faith is based around that baby and what He grew up to do, it is right and proper to ask why we would ever leave Him out of the picture, so to speak.

This provided a great way to discuss the Incarnation but it also prompted me to look at images of St Joseph, patron of fathers and a model for all fathers, biological and adoptive. A quick search on the internet or through books of images reveals different images of St Joseph in his many patron roles such as worker, happy death and father. It is remarkable how many of them don't have "the baby". It turns out that this is something of a historical phenomenon. Early icons and statues rarely, if ever, show St Joseph without the Christ child but as we move through the Middle Ages towards modern times we find increasing images of St Joseph as worker, contemplative or dying a happy death. So, even in the Church we find a developing image of the human father and, it would seem, that it is often a movement towards being removed from nurturing the infant in a direct way towards being a provider.

Father as patriarch

Perhaps one of the most enduring images of fatherhood in Scripture and society is that of the patriarch. In modern times the idea of a patriarch has come to be presented in very negative terms, suggesting control and even oppression. The term "patriarchal society" has become a way of suggesting failure in cultures or that they are somehow undeveloped. Whether we agree or not, it is a reality that the notion of patriarch is no longer one that is valued in our culture. This is perhaps not surprising as the term has become increasingly abused over the centuries to the point where it is now virtually unrecognisable from the biblical notions seen in figures such as Abraham. In Abraham and the other Old Testament patriarchs we find men with whom God deals directly and who worship Him faithfully. The God they worship is not one tied to a particular place or time but one who walks with His people at all times; these were nomadic people after all. The God of the patriarchs is one that we can have a personal relationship with and that is not bound to formal religious structures such as shrines or holy mountains. In short, He is a God that is in all places for all people. As nations became more linked to a particular land the idea of a patriarch as father of the people became associated with the king. This provided a softening of the idea that he ruled over people and pointed to a guiding and caring role.

What seems to have happened is that, rather than kings becoming more like fathers, fathers seem to have become more like kings in their own families. Fathers have increasingly expected to take decisions in a unilateral way, and to administer discipline and punishment in a household. Thus, rather than helping to soften rulers the term 'patriarch' seems to have contributed to hardening fathers. The image of a king is clearly one that modern fathers would do well to leave behind. Unilateral decision making devalues the role of the mother and wife, and denies the covenant bond of equals that exists in the sacrament of marriage. Obviously each marriage divides roles between the spouses differently but being a dictator in any area does no one any good. It is also important for fathers to remove themselves from the role of primary disciplinarians. Again, this is an area for joint responsibility. The days of "Wait 'til your father gets home" should be as far behind us as the times when a man arrived home expecting his dinner on the table and all the housework done by his wife. For one parent to be identified with discipline risks making them less approachable, the other a 'soft touch' and means that discipline is something that children can associate with something outside themselves. We do our children no favours if they do not learn that it will ultimately be them who will have to account for their own actions, and discipline themselves, as they become adults. If discipline is something Dad did, then when he is not around it doesn't apply. Perhaps one of the most common expressions of this is found in the loss of young adults from attendance at Mass. So many young people don't go to Mass because they associate it with childhood discipline, and see not attending Mass as an expression of their adulthood. I suspect we all know someone who still holds a faith but doesn't go to Mass regularly for these reasons yet, when they visit their parents, they attend Mass to keep their parents happy.

For a Catholic father today a recapturing of the image of the patriarchal father who helps his family to have a deep personal relationship with God, through His Church and all its gifts, is one that would be deeply helpful. Our children may then be helped towards a grown up relationship with others, with society and with God. The idea of the patriarch is one worth rehabilitating and one that would bring us closer to the image of the father in the story of the prodigal son. After all, the son in the story did not come to his transformation through authoritative discipline but through self-realisation of his errors in the face of unflinching love.

Shaping the Father

While we can see that fatherhood varies from culture to culture and changes over time, it will be news to nobody that no two fathers are the same. In fact, we often seem to decide on the way we will parent as much by deciding what we don't like about the way other fathers interact with their children as we do by taking on what we think is good. This probably applies most of all to our relationship with our own father and yet it is likely to be one of the most important experiences we have of fatherhood. However, the father we are is shaped by many things and I would like to look at three of them: our parents, our own choices and personality, and our children.

'They fill you with the faults they had'

It is important to be conscious of the influence our own parents have on our approach to parenthood. Not that we need to slavishly copy them, or avoid what they did, but to be aware that what we do now will influence our own children and their experiences as fathers and mothers. In his poem *This Be the Verse* Philip Larkin railed harshly against the impacts of his parents on his own life. The ripe language means much of it would be inappropriate to reproduce here, but the poem does contain the lines:

"They fill you with the faults they had
And add some extra, just for you".

And

"Man hands on misery to man.
It deepens like a coastal shelf.
Get out as early as you can,
And don't have any kids yourself."

Larkin is cynical and had a number of relationship problems himself, but the poem does touch on the fact that our decisions as fathers will go down the generations and echo in lives that we will never know. An enormous responsibility, yes; but unlike Larkin I believe it is also a wonderful God-given opportunity to do great things.

There comes a point in everyone's life when they need to stop blaming others for all of their failings and take responsibility for themselves. In short, we all grow up and however we are formed in childhood we retain the free will and intellect to make our own decisions. Becoming a father is probably one of the key moments in life, like the death of a parent, at which we are forced to face the challenge of being grown-up. Whether we rise to that challenge is up to us. The father we become is the product of our free choices made in response to events that we encounter. We are perhaps used to the idea of forming our conscience as part of our moral development and particularly in avoiding sin. I would like to suggest that something akin to this is required by each and every father as he prepares for the demands and opportunities of fatherhood. As we form our conscience we look for signs of sin and the occasion for sin, and seek to develop and nurture the virtues which will give us moral strength. As a father it is important to recognise the signs of problems, and the moments that "press our buttons" and cause us to stray from the father we want to be. Children do provoke us in a way that perhaps no other person ever can. We love them so much, we have such hopes for them and we feel we know what is best for them. We know that making mistakes is often the best way to learn but we don't want them to feel the pain that goes with it. Recognising, ahead of time, the points that make us become irrational or angry can not only prevent needless conflict but can enhance the relationship between us and our children.

The virtue of fatherhood

A virtue is a "habitual and firm disposition to do good", something that governs our acts and conduct "in accordance with reason and faith" (*CCC* 1833-1834). Although it is not listed as one of the virtues, fatherhood has all the characteristics of one. It is something where we seek the good of others, we seek to be reasonable and as Christians we seek to live in accordance with the faith. If we seek to nurture the virtues such as prudence which guides us to seek the true good; or justice which seeks to give each their due; or fortitude which guides us through difficulties; we prepare ourselves for the waves that crash on our shores as we go through life as a father.

But how do we nurture them? Yes, in prayer. Yes, through the sacraments. But, virtues are habits that are learned by doing them. To learn to be patient, or just, or prudent instinctively we need to practice them every day; even when it hurts. Just like going to the gym it is easy to drop out or subscribe but never turn up. That is why the communion and support brought through the Church acts to reveal God as our personal trainer, but we still need to listen. Only you know the areas that need working on and you know your strengths.

As with anything in life, fatherhood is best done if we play to our strengths and improve on our weaknesses, but this is no excuse to avoid the nasty jobs on the grounds that "I don't do that" whether it is nappies, homework or discipline. If you feel strongly about bedtimes, for example, and your children also feel strongly but in the opposite way it will achieve little to resort to conflict every night. Consider why you both feel strongly about it. You may simply want them out of your hair but they may wish to spend more time with you. You may still see them as very young but they may be feeling that they are growing up. Once you know why you differ there may be a simple solution that suits both you and them, such as allowing later nights at weekends and promising bedtime stories during the week. There is no end to the solutions but well formed habits and virtues will help us to consider a wider range of options rather than relying on confrontation and a culture of winning and losing.

Turning the tables

This, in many ways, brings us to the third key factor that forms us as fathers: our children. Each child is unique. Sometimes you wish they weren't, sometimes you are glad they are. Each is created in the image and likeness of God but bring with them an infinite variety of characteristics that require us to be a different type of father to each child. Sorry to say, but one size does not fit all. Perhaps one useful way of looking at this is to remember that each person is a unity, but also a complex of body, soul and spirit. Now, we have no difficulty with the diversity in physical appearance and talents. Some children are talented at sport, dancing or other physical activities whilst others seem to fall over at the least opportunity. Clearly, to force inappropriate activity on a child without talents or interest would be unfair and damaging to their self-esteem.

I really was the last to be picked for games at school and resented the teacher forming us into the inevitable line at games lessons and the humiliation that would bring. I had my revenge one day as I gasped around the cross-country circuit, last and with the teacher physically pushing me to stop me walking. As we crossed the line I turned to him in complete exhaustion and vomited over his shoes. It felt better than it sounds. We cannot expect our children to be the same as us and must never resent them for being different from us. If they are not the sportsperson you were then it is the father that must adapt and not the child that must be forced to change.

Whilst physical differences are obvious we must also remember that the same diversity exists in the other attributes that make up a person, their soul and spirit. The soul is the product of our heart, mind and will. Our emotions can be variable and unpredictable, our intellects vary hugely, and faced with the same set of circumstances our choices will not always be the same. In our spirit we are close to God, touching the divine; but just like our bodies it can be in varying degrees of fitness or even consciousness. The huge potential for variation in some or all of these factors is clear. We may know identical twins who look very similar but to find twins with the same personalities is unlikely in the extreme. Just as it would be wrong to treat twins as if they were the same person just because they look the same it would be wrong to treat our children identically just because they happened to be ours. As fathers we need to be adaptable, something that developing the virtue of fatherhood will prepare us for. One child may seek rough and tumble play, another may seek cuddles or more intellectual games. It is up to us as fathers to see that need and meet it rather than expect our children to change their whole personality to fit the type of father we are comfortable being.

If fatherhood is from God, shaped by Him and an opportunity to help make Him known in lives through the ages, it is not unreasonable to ask what guidance and help he has provided for this adventure which is clearly complex to say the least. Can we find anything of the essence of being a father in Scripture or the teachings of the Church? It is to this that we now turn and ask how good we are supposed to be at this seemingly superhuman task.

The Perfect Father

"Be perfect, as your heavenly Father is perfect." (*Mt* 5:48)

This short sentence must be one of the most daunting passages in the Gospel. In it Christ puts forward the universal call to holiness that applies to all Christians. The New Covenant brought by Christ continually challenges us not simply to obey His laws or to worship Him, but to be like Him. This we can do because he has redeemed us, allowing us to become adopted children who, like Christ Himself, can cry "Abba, Father" before God and become heirs to His kingdom (*Ga* 4:5-6). Now, we may well hold this to be true, and we may well believe that God has made us His adopted sons and daughters, but this does not take away the awesome nature of the call and the struggle that this entails. Indeed, the history of the Church is defined by this struggle to respond to the call for holiness. Many have succeeded in responding to this call in heroic ways. The canonised saints stand as beacons in our struggles and the countless other saints who remain unknown to us have also left a legacy in the society they have helped to form. Each one of us stands amidst a communion of saints that stretches through time and space, responding every moment to God's call for perfection.

So, what does this call to perfection mean for fathers? Are we called to be perfect fathers? Surely not, it is difficult enough to be half competent as a parent let alone perfect! Yet, elsewhere the call to perfection is repeated by St Paul, and linked to our adoption by God the Father through Jesus Christ (*Ep* 1:4-5). It is this call to perfection, I believe, that lies at the heart of fatherhood and why its downgrading by much of modern society is a loss to children, to society, and to men especially.

An experiment fuelled by psychobabble?

There is, it has to be said, already too much angst in our culture about being the perfect parent. A combination of factors combine to increase the sense of failure in mothers, fathers, grandparents and, ultimately, in children themselves. We live in a world that is increasingly comfortable with the concepts and language of psychology and these are frequently used to govern every aspect of our lives from shopping and driving to relationships and parenting. With the possible exception of statistics, psychology is perhaps the most abused of all the sciences. Television chat shows often engage in pseudo-psychotherapy, getting vulnerable people to express feelings and experiences in front of millions with what often seems to be the sole intent of causing conflict.

It seems virtually impossible to go to a party or a public meeting where psychological terms are not used freely, whether it is to do with selling houses or encouraging people to engage in worship. Nowhere has the abuse of psychology become more pervasive than in the area of parenting. Books, television programmes, newspapers and, perhaps worst of all, discussions with other parents, suggest that the mental health of children is being put at risk by appalling modern parenting or that if you use particular techniques you can get your children to do certain things. Sometimes it feels as if life is being turned into an experiment fuelled by half-informed populist 'psychobabble'.

Yet, there is something deeper within all of this. Fatherhood, like life in general, is a deeply spiritual experience; reflecting our creation in the image of God and our constant longing and search to be closer to him. For most people in modern society, religion has ceased to be part of their daily experience but they still strive to make sense of the spiritual dimension of life. As G.K. Chesterton once famously said: "When people stop believing in God they don't believe in nothing, they believe in anything". Psychological explanations have filled the gap left by the absence of religion for many people. One of the great challenges for the modern Catholic father is to guide his children in their search for the spiritual and to help them avoid the many false gods competing to fill the spiritual void that is often faced in today's culture.

So many false gods to worship

The false gods come in many forms, some apparently more benign than others. Most are reasonably harmless in themselves or in moderation but, just as in the story of the prodigal son, they often present an attractive path that leads us away from God, the loving Father, who gives us everything. So, fathers today are faced with: the pressures of popular culture and the cult of celebrity; expectation of academic achievement and testing; materialism and individualism; dispersed families and the loss of local community structures; fear of crime and 'stranger danger'; not to mention terrorism and environmental catastrophe amongst other global issues. Parents today find themselves working long hours to pay for housing and other needs, coming home to face pressures of homework and then find themselves chauffeuring their children to various social events because their friends live too far away or the traffic is too dangerous to let the children go by themselves. Surely it is enough to cause neurosis.

So many false gods to be worshipped and sacrificed to that today's father cannot begin to think of himself. Yet, that is exactly what he is doing in all of this. Unlike the prodigal son, it is not the children in this case that are worshipping the idols but the father. How often do parents stop and ask themselves why they are doing all these things? In all of these things we are often not meeting the needs, hopes or even desires of our children but, rather, ourselves. At the risk of straying into the realms of popular psychology, it is all too easy to find oneself competing with other parents or attempting to live out ambitions through our children. How many children care whether they are driven around in an old banger or the latest four-by-four, and if they do, where has that come from? A few weeks ago an eleven-year-old boy told me about how he wanted to go to Oxford University to study physics and that he was worried about passing the entrance exams for the school that would give him the best chance. These are not worries that have come from within the child, they have been learned from parents and others around him.

At the time of writing there is currently a credit card advertisement in which materialistic parents are 'sacked' by their children for failing to give them what they need. Their needs are shown as ways of spending time with children and giving them attention. The strap-line for the advert is "Remembering who you really work for: priceless". Inevitably, the solution proposed by the advert is to spend money using the card on activities with your children - it is trying to sell something after all. However, the sentiment is interesting as it challenges parents to reassess their focus, something we rarely do without some form of stimulus. When separating couples discuss the future arrangements for their children and their finances one of the first principles they are asked to subscribe to in negotiations is that the needs of the children are a priority. Invariably they agree with this principle, often saying that this is the sole reason they are present. There is something in parents that tells them that they must be prepared to make sacrifices for their children and to prioritise the needs of those who are unable to make decisions for themselves. Many do adhere to this, and they can significantly reduce conflict and aid progress by keeping sight of this horizon marked out by their children's needs. However, it is remarkable how many parents manage to conflate the children's needs with their own needs. In a spectacular illustration of the abuse of psychology the following argument is often worked through: "the most important person in a child's life is their mother/father and so it is important that I am happy in order for them to be happy". Just because you have children it does not mean that you cannot be happy or take into account your own needs, but what happens in this argument is the complete rejection of the notion of sacrifice or of prioritising children.

What happens in all that we have discussed in this section is the increasing degree of sacrifice made to false gods, the greatest perhaps being selfishness. These gods are not only hungry but are insatiable and ultimately demand the sacrifice of our children in the pursuit of self interest. In fact, what has happened in the above argument is that God has been removed from His rightful place as the most important relationship in a child's life and the parent has been inserted in His place. In doing this we venture dangerously close to the pride and vanity that is the epitome of sin.

Scriptural fatherhood

This may be a very dramatic way of putting it, but it is so far removed from the notion of fatherhood that we get from Scripture, and that is taught in our faith, that it is hard to avoid the parallels with the Fall of humanity in Adam, the pagan cults that Israel found itself struggling against in the Old Testament, or those faced by the early Church. What we cannot claim is that we have not been given any guidance in this matter; we know that it is wrong to try to replace the Father with the father. Let us not pretend, however, that these things are new. The problems facing fathers today are many and take new forms as technology develops and social norms shift but every age and place has had its pressures and false gods. This is because, ultimately, the choice to follow distractions and false idols comes from within; God has given us free will and, sadly, we often use that to turn away from Him. These pressures and challenges of fatherhood in any age should not be regarded as a cause for despair. They are, rather, a gift from God in His call to perfection. Just as each age and place has its challenges they also need fathers to respond with renewed ingenuity and, above all, love as they respond to their calling to be like the Father.

When St Paul reminds the Ephesians of the call to perfection as adopted sons of the Father he immediately follows the call with a reminder of the glory of God's grace which he has given to us to make perfection possible (*Ep* 1:5-14). In His wisdom, the Father has revealed the mystery of His plan for us and for the whole of creation. All things are to be brought together in perfection under Christ, a mystery that has been revealed to us in Christ and which we hear in His Gospel of salvation. Fatherhood falls within this greater picture of the grace of God and His infinite variety of gifts to draw us closer to Christ in whom the whole of creation can be made perfect. Fatherhood is not something we are called to be perfect at but is, on the contrary, a gift to help us grow towards perfection in the image of our Father in heaven. We need to look at this a little more and consider what this means for life as a father.

Fatherhood as Sacrament

As Catholics we are well used to the idea of God's grace and the ways in which He has given us opportunities to receive that grace. Above all it is the sacraments that we think of first when we consider grace. Sacraments are effective signs of grace: they confer the grace that they signify. They are not simply empty signs or symbols but are actions that actually make present to us Christ, who is at work in the sacrament. While there are seven sacraments in the Church many things in the life of the Church are sacramental in their nature. These take many forms from icons and holy water to hymns and blessings but they all work within what the Church calls the "sacramental economy" of salvation. Our salvation has been made possible because God has revealed Himself to us through Jesus Christ.

Fatherhood, too, is sacramental in its nature; making Christ present in the life of the man who lives out his fatherhood and reaching out into the family and beyond. The sacramentality of fatherhood makes sense only in the context of the sacramental economy which is available to the whole of humanity, and becomes clearer when we think of it in relation to the Church and the sacraments. Fatherhood is linked to all of the sacraments, as can be seen in the intimate link of fatherhood and reconciliation in the story of the prodigal son. However, three of the sacraments - Baptism, Eucharist and Marriage - help to provide special insight into the sacramental nature of fatherhood.

Baptism and the Eucharist

The sacrament of Baptism is fundamental to our membership of the Church and to our openness to the graces offered in all things sacramental; this will be considered in more depth later as we look at fatherhood as a key way in which men live out their Baptism. The Eucharist is the sacrament from which the whole life of the Church flows; nourishing each of us, binding us together, and making Christ present to us in a very special and real way. It is to the Eucharist that each father must keep returning to make sense of his calling in the sacrifice offered for the good of all and to give thanks for the graces received. The ultimate goal of any sacrament is to draw us towards communion with God through the gift of His grace and there is nowhere that this is made more present in this life than in the Eucharist.

A new horizon

In our struggle to understand what fatherhood is and how it should be lived out in our daily lives, the sacrament which provides the most concrete context must be Marriage. Clearly it cannot be argued that fatherhood can only exist within Marriage; there are too many examples around us every day to suggest that you cannot be a father without being married. Interestingly, until 2003 an unmarried father did not have automatic parental responsibility under English law and could only get such legal recognition if the child's mother agreed, or through a court order. Today, as long as his name is on the birth certificate he has equal standing with the mother, although for a married father it is automatic. Whilst this is a small quirk of English law it does suggest that, even in our largely secular society, the fullness of fatherhood is recognised as lying somewhere in the covenant between husband and wife, as well as a biological relationship and the emotional bond between father and child. Neither can we suggest that marriage without children is any less of a sacrament or that it contains fewer graces. Each marriage makes Christ present in the life of the couple, and those around them, in a unique way and presents countless opportunities for generosity and love. The point is, not that fatherhood or motherhood elevates marriage, but that marriage elevates parenthood to the sacramental level. My daughter is a great lover of all things chocolate. When she was younger she particularly loved one type of cake that was sold in the local supermarket and that we would buy from time-to-time when it was found in the 'reduced' basket at the end of the aisle. It was always thoroughly enjoyed. On her birthday I discussed with her about a cake for her tea with friends and she insisted that this was the cake that she really wanted; it was duly bought at full price. During the tea she hugged me and said that the cake was 'fantastic'. My reply was to point out that it was the same old cake we had eaten so many times before. "But it tastes so much nicer as a birthday cake" was her answer. Now, it is not that fatherhood just 'tastes' better within marriage but there can be little doubt that context can transform many things, including fatherhood. The theologian Karl Rahner often spoke of humanity living against a 'graced horizon' in which our whole existence was bathed in God's constant offer of Himself through grace. This horizon transforms human existence into an opportunity to respond to God's offer and grow closer to Him. In a similar and very particular way, marriage provides a graced horizon against which fatherhood can be lived. This does not mean that unmarried fathers cannot be just as good or loving as those that are married. Neither does it mean that married fathers are necessarily more competent or caring; just as people who receive the Eucharist are not necessarily 'good' people. What it does mean is that the wondrous gifts of fatherhood are enhanced and provide opportunity for insight, love and grace for the father himself. Fatherhood does involve generosity. It does involve sacrifice. However, above all things, fatherhood is a gift to the man who is living it; it is an opportunity for grace and love that elevates him towards the Father.

Set no bounds to your love

Fatherhood is, then, not something we are asked to be perfect at. It is something that aids us in our call to be perfect like the Father. As with all the sacraments, God is not bound in his generosity to the limits of our actions and experience. In the Second Vatican Council document on the Church, *Lumen Gentium*, the Council asserted that the gifts of God are not limited to the visible institutions of the Church but it is there that they are found in their fullness. You do not have to be a baptised member of the Church to receive God's grace and salvation but there is so much in the Church to help you that it is imperative that the Church makes this known to all. Similarly, you do not have to be a father to be perfect, but if you are a father you have been given a great opportunity to encounter God through your marriage and children and to grow in perfection.

We opened this section with a quotation from St Matthew's Gospel (5:48) taken from the Revised Standard Version of the Bible. An alternative translation, from The New Jerusalem Bible, perhaps provides some further insight:

"You must therefore set no bounds to your love, just as your heavenly Father sets none to His."

Fatherhood expands our horizons and increases our opportunities to love in a boundless and unselfish way just as the Father does. The challenge is to embrace this and to seek how to love unconditionally and generously, a truly heroic task in the age of distractions and false gods.

Being a Hero

"Dad!" said the small voice below me "You are brilliant, you can do anything!". The small voice was that of Luke, my son, and my heroic act was retrieving a small rubber-band powered plane from the roof of an outbuilding in our garden. I'm not very good with heights, to say the least, but even I couldn't claim that this was an act of heroism that any outside observer would acknowledge. Nonetheless, I felt like a hero simply because one little boy thought I was. Needless to say, since that day Luke's expectations of me have become a little more realistic but I don't think that his opinion of me, or my daughter's for that matter, have become any less important to me. But I am not under any delusions. Even as I stood there on the flat roof of the shed, basking in my sheer heroic manliness, a conversation of some years before returned to me and brought me back to Earth with a bump.

Pub wisdom

As a young man my conversations with friends in the pub, or slumped in front of the television eating takeaway food, rarely reached the heights of being coherent or sensible, let alone memorable. One evening as I returned with the drinks from the bar, doing the mental calculation to see if I could afford it if my round came up again, the conversation was unusually hushed around the table. Somehow, and it never became quite clear how, the conversation had drifted onto the subject of fathers. "When did you realise that your father wasn't perfect?" was the question that greeted me. Apparently, this experience is supposed to be seminal in each person's life. So the pub wisdom, fuelled by beer and a television programme, would have it. The hushed tone was due to a friend confessing that he had been beaten quite badly by his father as a child and that even with this it had taken him a long time to realise his father's imperfections. When he had realised his father's weaknesses it had brought a great sense of freedom.

I couldn't lay claim to any such trauma. It may be deeply unfashionable, but my childhood was happy. In his autobiography *Where Did it All Go Right* the journalist Andrew Collins contrasts his childhood with the misery portrayed in Philip Larkin's poem by stating "They tucked me up, my mum and dad". My childhood was one of being tucked up and so I don't remember any great moment of revelation regarding my father's less than godlike abilities. I suppose each minor ailment or badly executed DIY project brings with it a growing sense of vulnerability and fallibility. Eventually we all come to see that everyone in our lives, even our parents, are not perfect.

It is perhaps this that allows us to start to know them as people rather than simply our parents, and to grow up ourselves. Trying to be perfect for ever, to always be the hero in our children's lives is impossible and perhaps it isn't even really that desirable. One day, God willing, our children will be grown-ups too and as fathers we need to grow with them. I will always be able to revel in that moment of adoration as I stood on the shed roof but to seek to live in it all the time would not be healthy for me or my children. Our children have come to life through us and grow with our help. Almost without exception, as with my friend who endured beatings over many years, our children love us unquestioningly and unconditionally. They are central in our lives and we are central in theirs. But, we are not their destiny. We are not why they are here. We are not what they should be adoring. God is their destiny, their purpose and the true focus of their adoration. The job of a Christian father brings with it the task of drawing our children towards the true source and destiny of their lives.

The true hero of the parable of the Prodigal Son

The parable of the prodigal son is the ultimate example of this. It is not explicit in the parable but it is implicit, as with all of Jesus' stories, that the constant companion through all of the trials is God Himself. God calls His children to adventure, guides them and is ultimately the prize that is won.

An even clearer, and more complete, illustration of this is found if we step back and look at the whole story of the Bible. This is something worth doing. Often we hear or read small parts of the Bible but don't get an overall picture of the remarkable story that it tells. There are a number of translations of the Bible available now that do this and are well worth a read. Even better, children's Bibles often do this well as do some film animations available on DVD. I have often used these materials not only with children but also with adults preparing for reception into the Church, as a way of giving an introduction to the Bible, or to provoke discussions with those yet to become comfortable around traditional Scripture study. Often the emotion conveyed in dramatisations captures the essence of a passage very well and allows us to enter more deeply into the Scriptures when we read them. Reading or watching these together can be an excellent way of discovering the story of God and humanity with your children. After all, that is what the Bible is; the story of God and humanity, a father and His children. It is a love story without equal in which a loving father calls his children to live an adventure with Him, to go on a quest from which they will return with the prize of eternal life with Him.

The story begins with a loving Father who creates the universe as an expression of love; He doesn't have to but He does. At the pinnacle of this creation is humanity, created in the Father's image and likeness; destined to share in His eternal life and His work as co-creators. The Father's love is so complete that He takes the risk of allowing His children the freedom to make their own choices and to exercise their will, even if that is against Him. They do exercise this free will against Him and reject His love and gifts. This rejection is not inevitable but it happens all the same. What does the father do in response? Disown them? Punish them? No, he keeps loving them; reaching out and continually calling to them to return. Even in our darkest moments when we wander farthest from Him he is still there calling us back with open arms. The Father doesn't even expect the whole of humanity to answer Him with a single voice but is content to find a single man, Noah, Abraham, Moses or others who are prepared to listen to His call. Through these people He makes a Covenant with humanity. This Covenant goes beyond a mere contract, it is a bond or a marriage between God and humanity in which God promises to be ever faithful to us and asks us to be faithful to Him. God never breaks this Covenant but humanity does, time and time again.

Time and time again God renews His Covenant with humanity, giving laws to guide and prophets to teach but all are ignored. Eventually God makes a new Covenant with the whole of humanity through a perfect man, a man who is all that human beings are called to be. This man is God Himself, incarnate and present in the world; Jesus of Nazareth. He takes on all that it is to be human and by doing this makes it divine and reveals His total and unwavering love for His children. The bond made in this New Covenant cannot be broken by humanity because it is between the Father and His Son, who stand for all of humanity, and sealed in the Holy Spirit. In this New Covenant of love, humanity has been drawn into the very heart of the one God revealed to us as the Trinity. We have been on a journey, accompanied by God, and have returned with a prize that isn't simply eternal life but is life with God Himself as His sons and daughters. However, our free will remains. We cannot break the Covenant between God and humanity but we can choose as individuals whether we want to be faithful to it, or if we want to accept the gifts on offer. The Father's love is such that he still takes risks.

Taking risks

It is in this risk-taking father, driven only by love, that we find the perfect model of fatherhood. Again, it is daunting to be asked to be God; but that is not what is being asked. What is being asked of us as fathers is to take the risk of allowing our children to be the hero in their own stories. If we try to be their hero then they cannot grow, and neither can we. We need to love them enough to allow them to exercise their free will, to go on the quest that life offers them and to be there with open arms ready to run out and greet them on their return with the prize they have gained. Only by being the hero in their own lives can they be all that they are called to be. We cannot be the hero in their story nor can we expect them to be the hero in our story.

There is no doubt that this is scary. Are we being asked simply to abandon the most precious things we have to a world that does not care for them as we do? Of course not, our role as father is as companion on life's great adventure.

As the Church teaches, we are the first teachers and guides of our Children (see *CCC* 1653). It is in the home, beyond all other places that our children become who they are. It is in the family that they learn about relationships, morality and their faith more than anywhere else. This starts at the earliest of ages. Research increasingly shows that babies sense not only the way we interact with them but also the way we behave towards others. This only increases as they get older. Thus the Church rightly says that we must educate and guide our children in faith and morals from their "tenderest years" (*CCC* 2225). Our call to fatherhood, then, brings with it an obligation to reflect God's love in our relationship with our children but also with our wife, wider family, parish and all those we meet. Our task as companion starts from the very beginning of our children's lives and we are called to remain with them on that adventure until the end. Indeed, our belief in life everlasting and the communion of saints suggests that our companionships goes on even beyond our lives on earth. "To infinity and beyond" as the Toy Story character Buzz Lightyear would say.

But what does this mean for our call to perfection that we looked at above? As we mentioned, being a father is a blessing on the individual and on the marriage (*CCC* 1652). This is not some simple nicety but reflects the real grace that comes with parenthood as we are called to look beyond ourselves and to help another person grow, thrive and become another hero in the story of God and humanity. In the story within stories that is life, their victory elevates us to ours.

So, our children and the reality of parenthood open us up to grace and looking beyond ourselves. Even more than this, in becoming fathers we are called back to the moment at the creation of humanity itself where we stood in original grace and walked with God. As parents we co-operate with God in His continuous act of creation and gain a glimpse of what we were created for and what we are called to. But this is an heroic task in itself, a task that we need companionship and guidance for. Our companion is God, our challenge is to seek Him amidst this world of distractions and false gods.

The Unchanging Father

Being a father

Recently, after a lecture on the social teaching of the Church, I did what I frequently do and sat with some of the students, drank coffee and discussed matters relevant and irrelevant to the lecture. Almost out of the blue one young woman started to become highly emotional and said how happy she was to be on a course where people believed in absolute things. Relieved that I hadn't upset her, I asked why. Prior to joining the programme of study she had been at a different institution studying philosophy and had been laughed at in classes by students and staff for asserting her belief that absolute values and realities existed in this world, not least the reality of God. Relativism in modern thought is pervasive to say the least and has exercised the minds of many thinkers in the Church, not least just about every Pope over the last hundred years or more. Without wishing to produce caricatures, it can be said that those who take an extreme relativist position argue that not only are matters of morals, aesthetics or other values relative but that the nature of knowledge and even our own existence are only relative truths. Clearly, amongst many other things there is no room for God in such a world. Naturally the Church argues against this and some great arguments can be found in the teaching of John Paul II and Benedict XVI amongst others. But, are all things absolute in their nature? Does everything have a particular way it should be, should look or should be done? Is there a particular way we should be a father?

To answer this last question with a simple yes would be to misunderstand the argument against relativism. Acknowledging that there are absolute values or a natural law in the world does not mean that there cannot be diversity in its expression or even that diversity is essential to its expression. After all, we believe in one God and one Church but nobody can deny the huge and rich diversity in the way people around the world and through time have lived the Gospel message in service of God and man. If the Church had only expressed its unity in one uniform way it would probably never have reached all nations and would have remained an odd little group amongst the Jewish community of the Middle East. Just as with the Church, fatherhood in the image of the Father in heaven can take an infinite number of forms. But, this does not mean that there is not something that binds all fathers together and to which they must strive. Each Catholic father is called to live his mission as a man created in the image of God, as a husband and as a baptised Christian adopted as a son of the Father. How we do this will be governed by many factors.

What's in the word - 'father'

The Swiss linguist Ferdinand de Saussure was highly influential in the theory of language in the twentieth century and wrote from an essentially relativist position. He argued that words only had meaning because of the definitions given to them by a particular culture and time. Many cultures do not have equivalent words for the same thing he argued, so words do not relate to pre-existing realities. This does hold true for some things that do not come under universal human experience. For example there is little need for a word for 'freezing' if you live on a small tropical island. The word 'father', however, does have an equivalent in every language and it relates universally not only to what we might call the 'biological father' but to someone with a nurturing role in the life of an individual. In *Fatherhood Reclaimed* Adrienne Burgess describes a huge diversity in the way fatherhood is lived out around the world but in every culture the father is a central figure. The word, father, in whatever language, is not something that is determined by the culture we are in, or the words that surround it. The word father is a word that is lived and defined by the man living it. To say "I am your father", is to say "I will be your father; I will be whatever it takes to be your father". To be a father is to make a promise; something to be lived, rather than a statement of fact. This is perhaps why so many men find it hard to admit that they are the father of children conceived outside marriage or other relationships. A young man of nineteen, Kieron, once said to me, as he chewed his already worn down fingernails, that he couldn't be the father of the eight month old baby girl I had just seen with her mother. "But the DNA says otherwise, and the Child Support Agency won't believe otherwise now" was my naïve reply. "No" he said, "I mean I can't do it, it scares me". Unfortunately Kieron left his baby and did all he could not to "be" her father. I am sure many young mothers feel the same but cannot run away, or resort to abortion to avoid living 'their word'.

There is no doubt that being a father is a challenge as well as a joy, but without the scary bits any adventure would be very dull. The key is to remember that we are not alone. God has given us every grace and support that we need; we do have our companion on our heroic adventure. My mother-in-law has faced many tests in her life but meets each one with a certain faith and the belief that "God does not ask us to do anything that he doesn't also give us the strength for". She finds her strength in the Scriptures, in prayer and in the sacraments; but she doesn't simply turn to them in times of need. These things are her 'daily bread', fortifying her for whatever may come and her reserves are phenomenal for it. She has made a virtue of living, forming every aspect of her life to meet whatever comes her way. There can be no better food or preparation for the trials and challenges of fatherhood than these gifts, but there are others too. We find strength in our relationships, particularly in marriage. We find strength in hearing the stories and wisdom of others. These are all ways that our great companion guides us in our journey but we must be open to this at all times and not simply at times of need. "Being" a father, growing in fatherhood and fulfilling our promise, is not something that can be done when it suits us or looked for when the need arises. It is something that comes in the day-by-day living of life, a virtue practiced and a perfection sought. Where we choose to learn from is critical for the type of father we are and the example we pass on to our children and those around us.

There are many courses available these days that offer "parenting skills" and in their own way they are very good. They fill a growing gap that seems to have been created by the lack of good role models in parenting, especially amongst men. A drawback of this approach is that being a father is reduced to a set of management skills and techniques similar to those used to optimise performance in the workplace. Children are asked to subscribe to behaviour contracts, are offered incentives or faced with consequences and sanctions if their actions or performance is not up to scratch. Clearly these are things all parents do informally, with varying degrees of success. My reservation about much of the culture surrounding such "skills" is the reduction of children to a problem to be managed or an asset to optimise. This runs counter to the Christian 'personalism' that underpins Catholic social teaching which calls us to see each person as an individual made in the image of God; not as a problem or an asset.

Father to God's children

At the heart of being a father in a Catholic family is the realisation that our children are God's children. We are called not simply to love them as "ours" or "mine" but as His. There are few activities that give an insight to this as much as praying together as a family. We see our children building a relationship with their other, even more real, Father and can see that we are simply stewards called to make His love present to them. In their prayers they are often more honest than in talking to us. Listening to my children's prayers I have come to know about their cares and concerns from wobbly teeth to bullying and concerns in their minds raised by the break-up of other families. Faced with the honesty of their prayer my own often feels clumsy and dishonest. I feel that in talking to God with them they help me to grow in the call to perfection.

Finally, we must remember that in all that we do as a father we are sharing in something much greater than ourselves. God has spoken the words "I am your Father" (*Lk* 3:22; *P*   2:7), but His utterance was not a promise to become, to grow, to develop into a father. The Fatherhood of God just is; it is a fact that never wavers. This is what we can fix our sights on and aim towards, this will be our companion through our adventure. Ultimately there can be only one parenting skill, one tip or instruction in the handbook of fatherhood that never comes and it is found in the words of St Augustine: "Love - then do whatever you like".

The Role of a Christian Mother

Being a Mother is one of the most essential roles any woman can have, yet in today's world it has become one of the lowest status occupations, undervalued and under-rewarded. After summarising the physical, psychological and intellectual challenges of motherhood, Anna Melchior goes on to describe its rewards and gives useful tips and reflections which can help experienced Mums and Mums-to-be to value their role and its importance for the family, society and the Church.

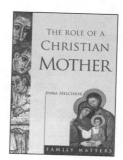

ISBN: 978 186082 533 0

CTS Code: PA12

The Family's Mission to Love

The family is where we learn the most important lessons of our life, and whatever our own family is like, it can still be a place where we learn love and forgiveness. This booklet gives case studies and practical tips on making the family a school of love not only for its members but also for the world outside. This booklet seeks to restore to families their dignity and sense of mission - to bring a love of Christ and of life itself to the whole world.

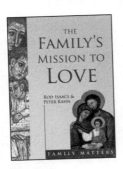

ISBN: 978 1 86082 464 7

CTS Code: PA10

Work and the Christian Family

In a time when life is becoming increasingly expensive and when long working hours are the norm, finding the right balance between the demands of work and of the family is a difficult task. This booklet identifies the most important elements of a work-life balance that allows time for children and space for a life of Faith.

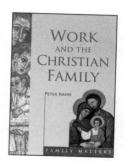

ISBN: 978 186082 634 4

CTS Code: PA14